Places of Worship

Izzi Howell

Raintree is an imprint of Capstone Global Library Limited, a company incorporated in England and Wales having its registered office at 264 Banbury Road, Oxford, OX2 7DY – Registered company number: 6695582

www.raintree.co.uk
myorders@raintree.co.uk

Produced for Raintree by
  White-Thomson Publishing
Edited by Izzi Howell
Designed by Rocket Design and Clare Nicholas
Picture research by Izzi Howell
Production by Kathy McColley
Originated by Capstone Global Library
Printed and bound in India

ISBN 978 1 4747 5394 4 (hb)   978-1-4747-5396-8 (pb)

British Library Cataloguing in Publication Data
A full catalogue record for this book is available from the British Library.

Acknowledgements
We would like to thank the following for permission to reproduce photographs:

Alamy: Hans Blossey, 6, Simon Balson, 14; Dreamstime: Brownm39, 30 (bottom), Draghicich, 8, Enriquecalvoal, 25, Jamie Frattarelli, 20, Masar1920, 24, Tupungato, 15 (bottom); Getty: Alain Le Bot, 16, Amanda Lewis, 10, esp_imaging, 4 (top left), FatCamera, 5, Feargus Cooney, 28, Gabi51, 30 (centre), Godong, 21, Gwengoat, 18, Huw Jones, 23, nadger, cover (top centre right), patty_c, 9, peterhowell, 22, ripmp4, 30 (top), stevenallan, 17, Ultima_Gaina, 4 (top right), umutkacar, 12; Shutterstock: Belozorova Elena, 27 (bottom), elvirchik abdrahmanova, 13, Christian Mueller, 7, Ilona Ignatova, 11, 1 Wei Huang, cover (bottom background), kaprik, 15 (top), kunanon, 29, Lizavetta, 19, Paul J Martin, 4 (bottom left), paul prescott, cover (top right), pingkung753, 1, 26, Sabrina Marchi, 27 (top), Shunsho, cover (bottom foreground), SmileStudio, cover (top centre left), Tom Gowanlock, 4 (bottom right), Tupungato, cover (top left).
Title page image is of Buddhapadipa Temple in London.

Every effort has been made to contact copyright holders of material reproduced in this book. Any omissions will be rectified in subsequent printings if notice is given to the publisher.

We would like to thank Dr Suzanne Owen, senior lecturer of Theology and Religious Studies at Leeds Trinity University, for her help in the preparation of this book.

Contents

Some words are shown in bold, **like this**. You can find out what they mean by looking in the glossary.

Introducing places of worship

The six religions with the most followers are Christianity, Islam, Judaism, Hinduism, Sikhism and Buddhism. People from these different religions **worship** in special buildings.

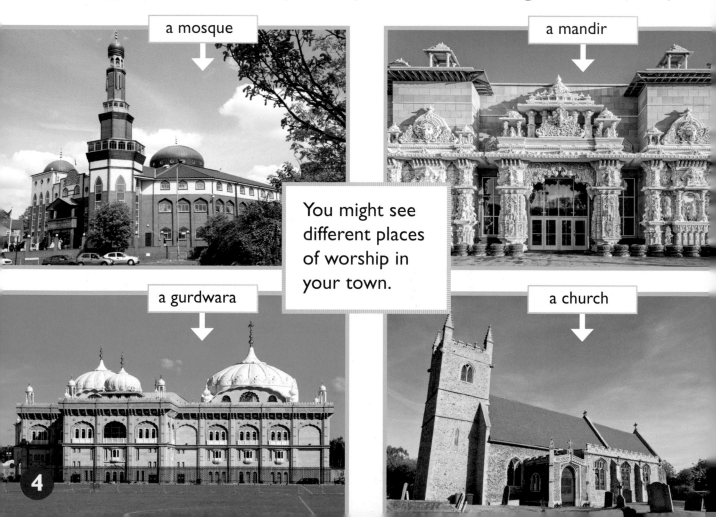

a mosque

a mandir

You might see different places of worship in your town.

a gurdwara

a church

People meet and celebrate in places of worship. They listen to religious leaders and share ideas.

These Christians are singing songs together in a church to praise God.

Churches

Churches are Christian places of **worship**. Some Christians go to church every Sunday. Others only visit at special times such as Easter or Christmas.

Some churches are cross-shaped. The cross is a Christian **symbol**. It reminds Christians of Jesus.

Churches can be small and plain or large and decorated. Cathedrals are large churches. Some churches and cathedrals were built hundreds of years ago. Some are very new.

Christians often build tall churches to **honour** God.

At the front of some churches, there is an **altar** with a Bible and a cross. The Bible is the Christian **holy** book. It teaches Christians how to live.

The altar is often decorated with flowers and candles.

Many churches have stained glass windows. The windows often show stories from the Bible.

In this church, the **priest** stands at the front of the church to lead the **service**. The people sit on rows of seats called pews. They listen to the priest.

Mosques

Muslims **worship** at home in a mosque. Some Muslims pray at the mosque five times a day. Muslims also go to the mosque to study and to celebrate festivals.

There is a **crescent**- shaped moon on this mosque. The crescent is a **symbol** of Islam.

crescent

Mosques often have a **minaret**. In some places, a crier calls from the minaret to call Muslims to prayer. In some mosques a recording of the call is played instead.

minaret (tower) →

Many mosques have curved **domes** on top. This mosque is in Dubai.

Muslims pray on the floor on mats.
They face an **arch** called the mihrab.
The mihrab marks the direction of
Mecca, the **holy** city for Muslims.

Men and women pray
in separate areas in
the mosque.

mihrab

There are no pictures or statues in mosques. Mosques are decorated with patterns and words from the Qur'an. The Qur'an is the Muslim holy book.

Muslims rest the Qur'an on a stand because it is a special book.

1899 5659 הק״ בית הכנסת
שער יעקב
FIELDGATE St G^t SYNAGOGUE

41

Synagogues are Jewish places of **worship**. Jews often visit the synagogue on the Sabbath. The Sabbath begins at nightfall on Friday evening and lasts until nightfall on Saturday.

Some synagogues are decorated with writing in Hebrew, a Jewish language.

You can see different Jewish **symbols** on a synagogue. One symbol is the six-pointed star, called the Star of David.

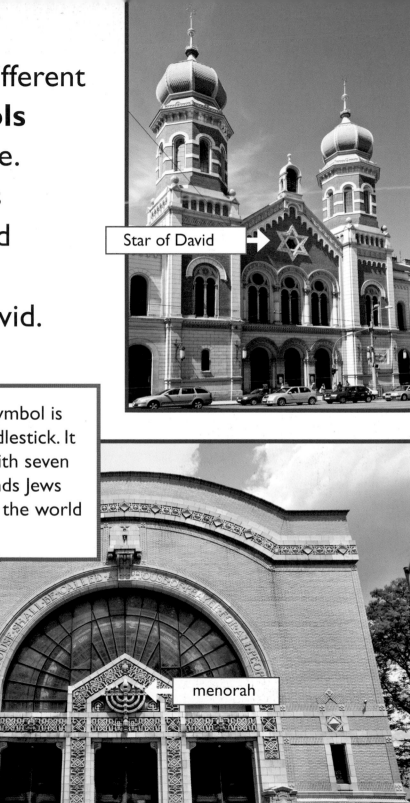

Star of David

Another Jewish symbol is the menorah candlestick. It is a candlestick with seven branches. It reminds Jews that God created the world in seven days.

menorah

Jewish people sit to listen to the **service**. They face a special cupboard called the Holy Ark. Inside, there are **scrolls** of the **Torah**. The Torah is the Jewish **holy** book.

In some synagogues, men and women sit separately.

Holy Ark

The **rabbi** takes the scrolls out of the Holy Ark during the service. Then he reads from them.

The Torah should only be touched with a pointer called a yad, because it is so special.

Mandirs

Hindus **worship** at mandirs. Hindu worship is called puja. Hindus perform puja whenever they can. They also worship at home.

Some mandirs have tall towers.

Many mandirs are made from stone. In some countries, the walls are decorated with patterns and characters from Hindu stories.

This mandir in India is decorated with **carved** Hindu gods and goddesses.

Hindus take off their shoes and ring a bell before they worship to tell God they have arrived. Hindus believe in one God but they have many different **images** to show God's different forms. There are colourful pictures and statues in the mandir.

Hindus pray in front of the images of God.

The images of God are decorated with flowers.

Hindus bring food and flowers to the mandir. The **priest** offers the gifts to the statues in a ceremony. Afterwards, everyone shares the food.

A gurdwara is where Sikhs go to **worship**. They usually go once a week. They celebrate religious festivals at the gurdwara.

There are always four doors into a gurdwara. The doors are a **symbol** that people from across the world are welcome.

The Sikh symbol is called a khanda.

There is a Sikh flag outside every gurdwara. The flag is orange with a Sikh symbol on it.

Sikhs kneel or sit on the floor to worship. They listen to a person called a Granthi read from the Guru Granth Sahib, their **holy** book.

Guru Granth Sahib

The Guru Granth Sahib is placed on a **platform**. It is treated like a special teacher.

There is a kitchen and a dining room in the gurdwara. Sikhs cook and eat a vegetarian meal together after the **service**. This is called langar.

Sikhs eat together to show that everyone is **equal**.

Viharas

Buddhists go to a vihara to **meditate**. They sit quietly and think. Buddhists do not **worship** a god.

Viharas often have a pointed roof.

There are often statues of the **Buddha** outside the vihara. The Buddha wrote the **holy** books of Buddhism.

Sometimes, parts of the vihara are decorated with gold.

Some viharas have an eight-spoked wheel decoration. This wheel is a **symbol** of Buddhism. It reminds people of the Buddha's teachings.

There are also **images** of the Buddha inside the vihara. Buddhists kneel in front of the images and meditate.

Buddhists show respect for the Buddha's teachings. They place flowers and candles in front of the images.

Buddhist **monks** live at the vihara. They study the Buddha's teachings. They also help other people to understand what he taught. Sometimes, Buddhist monks **chant** lines from holy Buddhist books. Buddhists say the words with them.

Some Buddhist monks wear bright orange robes.

Picture quiz

How much do you remember?
Find the answers on page 32.

1 Who worships here?

a) Jewish people

b) Christians

c) Sikhs

2 Where would you see this altar?

a) Gurdwara

b) Church

c) Synagogue

3 Which place of worship is shown here?

a) Church

b) Mosque

c) Vihara

Glossary

altar table used in religious ceremonies, often in a church

arch curved shape over an opening

Buddha person who started the Buddhist religion

carved cut from stone or wood

chant to sing or say words in a special way

crescent curved shape that is wide in the centre and narrow at the tips

dome curved, round roof

equal same

holy important to a religion

honour to show respect for someone

image something that represents something else. Some religions have images, such as pictures of statues, that represent God.

meditate to sit in silence and think calm thoughts

minaret tower on a mosque

monk religious man who spends his life studying religion

platform raised area

priest religious leader

rabbi Jewish religious leader

scroll long roll of paper with writing on it

service religious ceremony

symbol picture that represents a religion

worship to pray or take part in a religious ceremony

Find out more

Books

Religions Around the World series, Anita Ganeri (Raintree, 2018)

Following a Faith series, Cath Senker (Franklin Watts, 2018)

My Religion and Me series, Philip Blake (Franklin Watts, 2015)

Websites

www.bbc.co.uk/schools/religion/
Find out more about the religions mentioned in this book.

www.bbc.co.uk/guides/z297hv4
Explore the different parts of a mosque.

Index

Answers: 1) a; 2) b; 3) c